A Trip Through
Downer, Minnesota

A Trip Through Downer, Minnesota

Gretchen Johnson

LAMAR UNIVERSITY press

ISBN: 978-0-9911074-4-5
Library of Congress Control Number: 2014936803

Book Design: Theresa Ener
Manufactured in the United States

Lamar University Press
Beaumont, TX

Acknowledgments

Writing this book would not have been possible without my teachers and writing mentors—Joe Wenderoth, Bill Holm, and Adrian Louis. I am especially indebted to Roger Jones for his help with earlier drafts of many of these poems.

A special thanks goes to Naomi Shihab Nye for her words of encouragement on an earlier draft of this manuscript. Her kind words helped fuel my belief that this would be published.

Thanks to Theresa Ener and the rest of the staff at Lamar University Press for all their hard work on the book and for believing in this project.

Poetry from Lamar University Press

Alan Berecka, *With Our Baggage*
David Bowles, *Flower, Song, Dance*: Aztec *and Mayan*
  Poetry (a new translation)
Jerry Bradley, *Crownfeathers and Effigies*
William Virgil Davis, *The Bones Poems*
Jeffrey DeLotto, *Voices Writ in Sand*
Mimi Ferebee, *Wildfires and Atmospheric Memories*
Ken Hada, *Margaritas and Redfish*
Michelle Hartman, *Disenchanted and Disgruntled*
Lynn Hoggard, *Motherland, Stories and Poems from Louisiana*
Janet McCann, *The Crone at the Casino*
Erin Murphy, *Ancilla*
Dave Oliphant, *The Pilgrimage, Selected Poems: 1962-2012*
Carol Reposa, *Underground Musicians*
Carol Smallwood, *Water, Earth, Air, Fire, and Picket Fences*

Also by Gretchen Johnson:

The Joy of Deception and Other Stories

For more information on these and other Lamar Press Books go to
www.LamarUniversityPress.org

For my family

    Brian and Lois Johnson

    Alex, Jes, and Emmett Johnson

and dear friends

    Jen Nelmark and Kim Pehrson

I too saw the sun's first orange splash
out past the edge of town.

1

How to occupy a life in Downer, Minnesota:

Appreciate the nothingness,
spaces between emptied houses,
yellow grasses with bottle fragments
and broken plastic bodies
severed from old mower blades.

Learn to expect only
the delicious sting
of forgetting those browsing
at Henry's Hardware,
and make faces to speak to
in dust on tables.

Study the shapes in carpet
and the map found
in the ceiling texture,
bathe in taupe paint
to blend with your surroundings,
and always leave the door open
when you sleep
to let the breezes in from beyond.

2

"Be careful what you choose,"
boast the city folks,
but out here there is no choosing.
Pick A or A. That's it.

One café, one playground, one stop sign,
one gas pump, one highway, one school,
one mill, one bar, one graveyard,
one bank, one faith, one view,

so I learned the art of not choosing early,
studied hard, and made myself
a young professor of contentment
and was ready at twenty-eight to permanently plant my life
in that stationary spot behind the register
at my mother's Fabric and Fancies store,

and when Charlene asked me out, I went,
not because I wanted to
but because I never learned that seemingly selfish skill,
the skill that could have saved me—
the power of saying no.

3

The old Lutheran church three miles east of town
closed last week,
and, for the first time in ten years, the pews were packed,
everyone wanting a last taste of an era soon forgotten,

and after the service, one by one,
they stood at the old cedar pulpit
and told stories of a structure soon demolished
by neglect and changing times.

Elsie Gustafson nervously ran her wrinkled fingers
down the pulpit grooves
as she spoke fondly of Ray Chandler, an old man now,
but once her naughtiest Sunday School student,

and George Clayburn nodded sternly and chuckled low
as he recounted the rummage sale of '76
when the power went out and a knocked-over candle
burned all the loot and half the sanctuary.
"But this pulpit, and the whole altar was saved," he boomed.
"Before these god-damned corporate farmers came in
and wrecked it all."

And Shirley Mayvern shook and cried
and spread her arms out in a way too dramatic for Lutherans
as she walked down the aisle from the back pew forward,
the same steps traveled forty years before on her wedding day,

and when it was all over, we sat silent for a while
until, one by one, we left the little church,
each carrying an item or two out.
I grabbed an armful of hymnals
while Charlene pulled the portrait of the first pastor off the wall,
and we stacked all the contents of the old church out on the lawn
to be carried away to charity auctions and onward
onto the path that old dreams always travel to obscurity.

Pastor Claude was the last one out,
like an old woman frozen in her doorframe
before walking out of her farmhouse a last time,
and he shook our hands and invited us to the potluck
in the basement of the Methodist church in town
where we ate hot-dish and lemon bars
while the cranes came to pull the old church down.

4

One woman wanders these streets,
searching in the shadows of familiar faces
for the children she never had.

She mixes and matches angles and colors—
a nose here, a mouth there,
full flush cheeks, and searching eyes—
creating a collage of the child she'll never meet.

She understands that sometimes the unlived lives
are more important
than those who shuffle asleep over sidewalks
and only respond to the sound of their own names,

and she knows that the accumulation of Xs
on calendar days since her last period
serve as proof that the names she once chose
will only be spoken by strangers.

The old Lutheran church three miles east of town closed last week.

5

This town is for the young ones—
the fresh-eyed child who sees possibilities
in abandoned railroad tracks and discarded stacks of sticks
sitting on burn piles after a storm came through.

This town is for the old ones—
the man who sits at a winter window
patient enough to notice how the growing frost
looks like crystal palm leaves pressed against the pane
and for his wife brewing coffee in the kitchen while studying
the sculpture of icicles cradling the mid-morning sky,

but I am in the middle,
too old to invent magic in the everyday
and too young to realize it was there all along.

6

Layers of red maple buds
exist above me, so why have I never
seen the exact burst
of a leaf popping out?

I spent childhood hours staring,
waiting for the merging
of sight and expansion,

but nothing unhinged for my eyes,
life being too fast to disrupt stillness.

7

This morning, before sleep,
I watched the world wake up
and decided this one day I would stop
trying to be someone else.
Why be the first to rise
and not the last to set?

I too saw the sun's first orange splash
out past the edge of town
and the procession of lights
illuminating rooms in familiar houses,

but I will keep the spark of waking
behind my eyes. Evening and daybreak
will burn together inside me.

8

My mother finds light in Charlene,
says it shines out of her crevices
and strikes surfaces with its dull glow
as she moves from room to room,
says I force my eyes to focus on the wrong corners,

so I look for clouded angles,
for muted colors amidst black hair,
red elbows, and manure eyes,
but even the faded freckles
strewn across her neck
heave themselves toward me
with every muffled breath she takes.

9

Every year when the earth is full
with the smell of rotting leaves and manure
and the house on Highway 10 has faded a little more—
chipped paint and weakening floorboards
from another summer's harsh conditions—
I remember the year Grandma Jane's farmhouse
held us after her funeral,
her last brushing against August air.

She had planned a social gathering
before the inconvenience of not waking from sleep,
so we ate the flatbread prepared by her hands,
tasted the ingredients she sifted together and rolled out.

Uncle Ned cowered in the corner,
crumbling pieces in his rough hands,
unable to consume the bread she had touched,
unable to devour oil from her hands
or some of her dust sifted in.

I put a piece in my pocket
and carried it around a few days,
but in the end we always get hungry.
We always devour the flavor of the dead.

I remember the year Grandma Jane's farmhouse
held us after her funeral.

10

Today I saw an old man walking
with a young dog,
and I wondered what they'll do
when the other is no longer here,
the dog having no one to feed him
and the man no one to walk toward.

11

You must taste sunlight
and suck the sap
from violets and orchids
knowing you are unglazed
on your own.

Touch insecticides
to die a little each day,
and after blooming
thrive on gravel and mold.

12

Charlene has married many in her mind,
plucked men from fields
before growth completed
leaving each to replant
and search again
with damaged roots.

Now she licks away
years of drought and flood,
removes mud and dust left behind,
and makes this tree her own.

13

Corn stands high this summer,
so young parents line up their children for photos
to compare the towering stalks to their still small statures,
to try to hold that moment long after it escapes them,

and sometimes we all believe possessing is possible,
that the daughter in the photograph will remain
just as she is, her stare sewn tightly into the bright fabric
of a late August day, her tangled silken strands
caught forever in mid-flutter from a passing prairie breeze,

but soon the stalks will be plowed under,
fields bare and brown, ready for another winter,
and the houses too, though seemingly solid
and standing strong against the winter winds,
will one day not be there,

and autumn reminds us natives of the north
to look a little harder, stay outside a little longer,
to run freely through field rows and down gravel driveways,
to press palms against leaves and grass before snow arrives,
to see the child before she isn't there.

14

This morning I watched periwinkle
clear deadness away
from the sculptor's horizon at dawn.

Charlene sang as my pulse beat hardest
in the places my feet are sanded down
to almost nothing, a garden city over-tilled,

and I realized the maintenance men may never come
to fix my washing machine's broken motor,
while the baskets of clothes in the garage pile high
giving snakes a place to sleep,

and I understood that even the calypso singer,
waking up in Trinidad, finds emptiness
as an unknown melody marches on.

Three miles north of town it stands –
surrounded on all sides by yellow rusted grasses,
abandoned corn cribs and gravel roads –
a portrait of one man's vision, the barn with the smiling face

15

As these days of warmth begin to wane, I wait
for the voices to drop out, gradually at first—
a few clarinets and piccolos from the trees
followed by the fading of blooming
oboes a few measures later,

and as the days dissolve toward winter
each verse consists of fewer parts—
finger cymbals colliding on the branches
drift soundlessly a few beats and exit the piece
with a muffled departure note,
and the arpeggios of Spanish guitars hidden in rain storms
make their final appearance.

The bass is the last to go,
a constant rhythmic thumping.
Shoes and bicycles and the padded feet
of animals on pavement crescendo and quickly depart.

The orchestra then becomes the audience,
listening for the occasional pan flute solo
surrounded by silence as wind meanders
and twists across roads and through the sleeping fields.

16

One woman accumulates disposable goods,
fills her house and storage shed with bottles, boxes, and cans
to stock and save for the final years—
53 shampoos, 49 yellow sponges, 68 laundry soaps,
16 tubes of toothpaste, 70 boxes of trash bags,
39 bars of soap, 87 rolls of paper towels,
42 rolls of deodorant, and 96 razors.

Her house is a store with only one customer,
believing she will live as long
as there are products left to use,
but we wonder where all the merchandise will go
when her body too has exhausted its worth.

17

Three miles north of town it stands—
surrounded on all sides by yellow rusted grasses,
abandoned corn cribs and gravel roads—
a portrait of one man's vision, the barn with the smiling face.

Today, as autumn unravels, leaving each thread
of diluted complexion to awaken the snow,
I find myself staring at the smiling barn,
faded red panels and the lips that extend
far beyond the double doors,
and for the first time I want to go in,
to peer out of the nose through the hay loft
or pile hay high to see through
the windows of the eyes.

In dusk's dying light this barn is new again.
Fading cherry paint stands against
the confusion on a stranger's face years ago
when Algot Magner's brush composed a place
for us to sustain and return to.

18

Outside it is October,
and somewhere a blanket of black birds
settles over a parking lot
for these late hours
after shoppers have found homes.

Outside it is snowing,
but somewhere a man swims,
inhales the mist and warmth
of night's exhale.

Outside no one speaks,
so somewhere the voices settle;
they scuttle and scream and stammer
in cities that breathe all night.

Outside it is October,
and I am in the middle of being
forty-two, and somewhere a woman
blows up blue balloons to celebrate
nothing, only to see them in each corner
and calm these cold hours before morning.

19

I tried to leave once,
spent a month in a motel in Mitchell, South Dakota,
giving tours of the Corn Palace,
seeing faces of the world pass through
while searching for my own on the walls of corn,
rows of golden hues nestled against each other.

At night in my motel room
my voice became the domes calling across miles.
My eyes flickered toward the husks above the bed
as South Dakota flags ushered in humanity's pulse,

but when harvest time came
the palace was transformed
from a grandiose monument of rural ideals
to a plain basketball arena,
so I gathered a few grains from each hue
and headed home.

And I can feel myself driving south
through Pipestone and down 75 past Rock Rapids, Iowa,
watching the sun rise over foreign fields
as Charlene sleeps to dawn.

20

Charlene's love is warm
and constricting, lying awake beside me.

Her love is the tiny bugs in my eyebrows
scavenging discarded pieces of me,

each nibble an unwanted moment
of sweat on skin, midnight to noon
here in this bed
unable to remove her
but plucking away each hair,

each invisible insect of her breath,
each sting of every biting,
of every hour, of every invading movement
pulling us toward a house of vacancy.

21

People here are grass shoots
growing through cracked spaces
of a land paved over.

One man wears a shirt from Climax, Minnesota,
ten bold black reasons why life there is good
clinging to his back,
but he never moves.

He knows the apartment will preserve better
without his dust and decay,
and the job he never pursued
will settle in comfortably to a man
he once spotted in Georgia's Diner.

Washing the shirt inside out is enough,
and when the letters do begin to fade
the unlived routine will be mapped in his mind,
every gray word replaced
with a stale shining.

22

Charlene bathes for the bubbles,
bursts of air pockets meandering,
tingling through mazes of twisted
and tightly restrained hair
submerged under a cool sheet of water,

says it reminds her of the summer
when locusts covered the land,
and she was too young to remain indoors,
and her hair hung loose across grasses,
legs and dusty toes sprawled out for the sun,

and she welcomed the little legs,
the herd of strangers searching
through her hair, those layers of dark waves,
for something she couldn't give,
and she felt the land shifting
with each sensation as they moved over
and through her.

23

Ralph and Gail Josephson have one yellow bowl
shoved to the back of the cupboard, a wedding gift
unable to match the winter white pattern
of the others. It has moved from house to house,
never used, never filled with lettuce leaves
or steaming noodle soup, an unsightly embarrassment
to the ordered life they carefully chose.

The couple needs white's contrast,
a clear separation between colorful nourishment
and what holds it. They cannot live
a life that allows one yellow bowl.

24

Sometimes, in the middle of the night,
I pack a suitcase in my mind,
softly sliding shirts and slacks, socks and shaving cream
into the dusty suitcase while Charlene snores in the next room,

and as I sit alone in the quiet living room,
stuck on the sofa with a cup of powdered cocoa in hand,
my finger follows highlighted highways
across state maps spread out over the coffee table,
and I can feel myself driving south
through Pipestone and down 75 past Rock Rapids, Iowa,
watching the sun rise over foreign fields
as Charlene sleeps to dawn,

but I always rinse the cup out, fold the maps,
and head back to bed, and Charlene always wakes before me
and plans another day out too swiftly
for me to ever escape it.

One man drives north thirty-four miles every day
to feed the ducks at Wild Rice River.

25

My whole life is the dream
of an old man.
Friends drive by
whom I've never met.
My legs twitch,
knowing I will take up running
two years from now,
waiting for that first step.

I catch flashes: unbuilt house,
a frame that will hold me
as the fields sprout, swell,
and sink into the earth again,
and I study my mother's skin,
knowing it will be important,

but morning never comes.
Voices drift through
these sleeping days,
and sickness remains always
a few breaths beyond this.

26

Charlene is a night sweater.
Mornings, after she leaves for work,
I trace the sweat stained outline
of her body, thankful it will fade
as hours sip the sketch
and leave only her scent—
pickles and decaying leaves.

Like a child painting with water
on sidewalks and driveways
she can only invade sight
as long as her imprint presses itself
against my evaporation.

27

One man drives north thirty-four miles every day
to feed the ducks at Wild Rice River.
They're always ready for him
when the car pulls up and he unloads the loaves—
five white, two wheat, and sometimes a rye.

They've stopped migrating south,
knowing he will be there with food
even when snow drifts high over County Road 9.

When I see him buying bread at Gordon's Grocery,
now a man of eighty-two, not many winters left,
I wonder how many days they will wait
after his last visit.

28

One woman felt empty at fifty
until she had a tapeworm,
vibrant and bustling inside her.
She told her friends
she was eating for two

and refused to let the doctors remove him,
feeling at last maternal, a life without
finally full despite the ache of him eating away
her inner organs.

The day her weakness became too great
she felt a sense of loss,
clutched her skin and listened for movement,
a mother birthing a thing to be destroyed,
beaten and discarded before her.

29

Charlene is destroying me,
too slowly for anyone to notice,
like the Mount Rushmore t-shirt
worn and washed too many times,
the image of faces fading gradually
until mouths and eyes have dissolved completely
into the gray backdrop of fabric behind them,

and she says she loves me
as she moves out my black lab who scares her,
packs away framed photos of turkey hunts,
bowling trophies from sixth grade,
and the plaid wallpaper I installed myself,

and she says she loves me
as she shears my hair too short for January air,
talks endlessly through the last lunches with my mother,
spends nights uninvited,
and insists I shower with rose scented soaps,

and sometimes I stand alone
in my fast fading house and wonder
how many washes are left
before I fade completely.

I never really knew my father.
He was nearly seventy the day I was born.

30

I never really knew my father.
He was nearly seventy the day I was born,
so the days that made up what he called his good-living years
had already been plowed into past harvests
before mine had begun.

In seventh grade, when asked to write a paper describing him,
I wrote of math, of the constant counting up of years
that sat at the bottom of a chasm between us,
of times when I stayed in bed late
trying to somehow subtract our spreading separation,

but no matter how many times I worked the equation
the answer stayed the same.
Each time I took a step toward life
he took a step away from his,

so I learned to hate birthdays,
to hate those days leading up to the celebration,
days when my mother strung banners and balloons
across white walls
and ushered in relatives and friends to sing me one year older.
I wanted to somehow get stuck
in the fleeting position of early youth,
to stay there with him before the next season clicked over,
to be like a southerner and possess the ecstasy
of an endless summer.

31

Lately, I'm thinking about faces,
their simple intricacies and how they never leave me.
I see myself years from now in a store in Western Idaho
with these faces still surrounding my eyes
and blocking the ability for new ones
to make a fair impression.

Karen Manley's notched nose
will find me on a stranger's face
three years after she is buried
in the cemetery north of town,
and Clark Youngquist's flashy smile
will rest on the faces of every politician
when elections roll through town.

I wonder if my grandmother ever saw me
or if she was too bombarded with old, dead faces
to take in the new ones.

32

Charlene sleeps in cloud pants,
pale blue, puffed white, stars and moons,
huge expanses of sky across her ass,
fabric thin and stretched across thick thighs,
and a label that reads *Ruby's Sexy Sleepwear*
sewn into the seam across the back.

I hate these pants, hate her for wearing them,
but sometimes, when her talking stops,
and the house is quiet, I rest my head in the place
where cloud and star meet and stay there until morning.

33

I will never say that it will be sleeting
in Bismarck the day I die
or that wind will carry strands of my hair
across the miles to Cheyenne and Springfield.
I will never say that the peach floral fabric
I sold this morning will rest in the middle
of a quilt years after this store is closed
or that my carefully preserved skin and teeth
will decay any slower than the man
in the grave across the way,

but I know there will be corners of this house not covered
when the new tenants move in, a few nail holes
left unfilled, places where pictures of her hung willfully,
and the forgotten wire hanger will hold a stranger's lilac sweater
and stretch the shoulders to fit my form.

34

Two hours before the sun came up, I caught Charlene
staring at the ceiling fan's slow rotation
and tracing rows across her stomach,
cultivating the spaces between wheat colored hairs.

The dim glow of hours before morning
held back the weathered land of her face,
and the artificial breezes blew away years
of plucking weeds meant to grow taller than surrounding crops,
and for a moment the wildness of her eyebrows was beautiful.

I tried to follow the shadowing patterns of fan blades
or coax myself into sleep by stroking the back of my thighs,
but each time she blinked with so much emphasis
I knew we could only destroy each other.

So I waited patiently for the storm to blow over,
a man hunkered down in an empty basement
waiting for the tornado above to dissipate or pass over,
but it never did.

35

This fabric store becomes an opening
as snow shatters daylight
and creates a dimness beyond my window,
and I am the man trapped in the fold of imagining,
drifting through aisles filled with bolts of mustard velvet,
yards of silver crushed metal, and folded lace
on a shelf in back always overlooked.

I smell the sage corduroy
and blow warm air into the spaces
between wales, expecting the cloth to grow.

I press peach satin to my eyelids
and become a browser searching
through strangers in a Turkish street market.

I wrap sky colored ribbon around my thick waist
and glide past boxes of buttons and rows of thread
toward a bride standing in snow.

Today no one will venture this far out of town,
into the blinding white of this April blizzard,
to purchase a scrap of silk, a row of needles,
or to look for the man trapped in the fold of fabrics.

36

The night my mother died
the wind blew in from Wolverton,
carrying wisps of corn hair
to her yard and windows,

and it was as if she slept,
her body still dressed in a red night gown,
the fabric even twisted around her middle,
off-center from her last turning.

37

After my mother's death, Charlene was there,
a shining light in the darkness, they said,
but they were wrong.

Day after day she stood beside me,
her presence a dark pit within the outer circle of grief,
spreading out, taking over, filling my house and my life,
destroying the destroyed, like looters throwing bricks
through the windows of houses
floodwaters have already consumed,

so I waited patiently for the storm to blow over,
a man hunkered down in an empty basement
waiting for the tornado above to dissipate or pass over,
but it never did.

Instead she strengthened, moving my furniture around,
bringing in perfumes and candles, sweaters and socks,
covering my coffee table with handmade wicker baskets
and my bookshelf with stacks of wedding magazines,

and because I never learned how to stop the still swirling storm,
I surrendered to it,
sat down on my old green couch for a last time,
and watched as Charlene moved in.

38

Enclose your life within two population signs:
Welcome to Downer and *Now Leaving Downer*
Please Come Again.

Eat only what can be found in the five aisles
of Gordon's Grocery, and learn to wear
the blue sweater you bought
at the church rummage sale,
the same sweater Algot's children plucked
from his closet the week following his death,
the same sweater he wore every Monday
to the Post Office and even one Christmas
when it was still new.
Read only the books that travel through town
once a month on the mobile library.
Photograph the family in your own yard,
and make an afghan tent to camp out
in the wilds of your living room.
Notice the way Nita Hallstrom's short stature
slowly shreds the bottom seam of her jeans
and how Ross Erikson's voice cracks hardest
on mornings after the Vikings lose.

Turn off the TV, and spend spring Sundays watching
the slow surrender of winter hours,
the yearly battle where sun always defeats snow,

and memorize the names of birds who pass through
on their way beyond the city limits.

You'll be surprised
how much there is to see.

And memorize the names of birds who pass through
on their way beyond the city limits.

39

I haven't left my house in two days
after putting up the hand-written closed sign
at the store for those who don't know
and peeling all my fingernails back
to the place they were when I was still
under her skin.

I haven't showered or shaved or put on fresh clothes
because I know how to move when her voice is fixed,
when it is steadied between bookcases and bed-frames,
but today is confined
to the weightlessness of my mother's death.

I've smiled and discussed road conditions
with those bringing hot-dishes and fudge bars,
knowing when they return in three days
to collect the empty pans
they should be emptied and washed and ready
for the next desolation.

40

Winter is among us.
My hands have not felt night air
in months, and Charlene's cracked heels
remain stockinged even during sex,

and in these moments I almost
love her, almost love the way she moves
dust from cheese puffs and dry skin
around my house and the painful way her voice
vibrates through tiny holes in my teeth,
almost love the absence of my own voice
as she pins pictures of her presence
on every empty surface
and thrashes around in bed, trying to get comfortable,

but as winter wanes
and my frozen mouth begins to melt,
she will still be here.
When the picture edges curl
and white flannel sheets have pilled
on her side from too much turning
and sofa pillows are stained orange
from habitual late-night snacking,
she will still be here.
When her exposed heels dig
raw patches across my legs
and my voice can no longer be heard
and nothing is my own,
she will still be here.

41

One woman lived a year in Las Vegas
but never felt it,
never sucked in the steam
or held the hand of neon
until it exploded in her palm.

Instead her feet stayed covered,
afraid of pavement's summer sting,
and found their way back
to Downer, where music is always
slightly under pitch,
and she hums along never noticing.

42

Follow your dreams, they say,
but no one talks about the dreamless ones,
the folks who arrive at their funerals early
and settle in comfortably to the coffin in the side room
to wait for the long line of onlookers who will one day arrive,

or the ones who pave over the road to freedom
with piles of possessions—
mountains of musty magazines,
sheds stuffed and stacked with rusty tools,
bloated basements bursting with rummage sale relics,
and kitchen cupboards so swollen they rarely stay shut
in these houses heaped too high for the plow to empty them,

or the confused ones who never learn
the intricacies of their own minds,
like a man living for years with a spouse
speaking a different language
they nod in agreement to everyone around them,
and even their dreams are a collage of ideas spoken by others,

or the frozen ones, always waiting for spring thaw to free them
as clocks tick away years, always skipping summer,
their growth forever halted like the arctic willow
with branches hunched close to the earth, never rising
more than a few inches from where he started,

so follow your dreams, they say,
but they never talk about the dreamless ones,

the ones, like me, who sit and wait for the ideas to arrive, all the while knowing that they never will.

Winter is among us.

43

Sometimes I drive my old car out past the population sign,
past Sullivan Jones' dilapidated farmhouse,
and the railroad tracks that run from Warren to Graceville,
out where the midday moon stands slightly visible
inside a frame of weather worn telephone wires and posts,
way out where the road turns to gravel
and even the water tower fades from view.

And when I get there, I pull the car over, shut the engine off,
step out, and shout madly
into the emptiness of a treeless horizon,
shout all the things I cannot say—that I don't love Charlene,
that I want to sell the store and leave town,
that I want to quit church board and men's pancake club.

I try to shout loudly enough for the people of town
to feel the faint vibrations of my voice under feet,
hidden somewhere in fields and floorboards.
I heave and holler until my voice grows hoarse
and then head home, back to the stage of silence.

44

Sandra Nygaard travels to Split Rock Lighthouse
out at the edge of Two Harbors, Minnesota,
to scatter the ashes of her dead husband.
She drives all morning until she sees it—
a building of light standing taller than the cliff supporting it.

This is winter, and only those in search of solitude come,
only those who wish to walk with snow stung ankles
and feel the arrival of wind's long journey across Lake Superior.

She comes carrying the burnt remnants in a black box,
moves deep into the tree maze and up toward the descent.
She comes so that when the box is opened and tipped
and his ashes float out on the endless expanse of waves
where this lighthouse sends a constant beam
she will see a new light
shining out on the wide horizon of water.

45

Night spills over smiling teakettles
and the crescendo of shutting windows
from Sheboygan to Downer and westward
to Rapid City, and someday I will go there,
will stand against the opening of wildness
and feel the sudden shifts of weather,
wind roaring through Wyoming plains
and into South Dakota.

Grover Harris says wind blows harder here,
turns off his television in a huff
each time Chicago is called "windy city,"
says those folks should stand on his old field
on days when the wind whips up,
scuttles and scurries across the prairie in long waves,
days when winds harvest settled snow,
and outside only white can be found.

46

Winter nights when the temperature travels far below zero
and frost forms on the interior side of windows,
I pull wool socks and heavy boots over my feet
and button up the big fur-lined cow-hide coat,
turn off the back porch light and trudge out
through thigh-thick snow drifted up against the house,

and it is in these moments of greatest misery
when I love this place the most,
moments when each inhale bites the back of my nose
and the skin over my knees stings
even under three layers of fabric,
moments when wind chills approach negative fifty
and people and animals are huddled somewhere
hidden from view

because on these nights when the air is so dry
that even the memory of cloud cover has evaporated
and the steam from my warm exhale disappears quickly,
the stars standing in dark fields of beauty
seem closer than normal, so close
that if I had the longest ladder from the backroom at the store
I could step right into their shining.

47

I keep telling myself, tomorrow,
tomorrow she should leave,
and on Tuesday nights
sitting beside Charlene on the new floral couch
I repeat this in my head as Wheel of Fortune
tries to entertain us,
hoping her frazzled black hair
will leave, stop hiding in corners,
between pages in unfinished books,
and behind the sink where sponges never go,
but the words remain somewhere behind
these tired walls, behind my ability to say
what will be heard.
She remains a familiar piece
I can't remove
from the crevices of this house.

Sandra Nygaard travels to Split Rock Lighthouse
out at the edge of Two Harbors, Minnesota,
to scatter the ashes of her dead husband.

48

Maybe my nose needs to be rubbed
in the smell of her,
like a dog learning not to piss
on the new white carpet.

If one part of my senses
can sway the others into submission
she can be shut out,
a rabid animal running through darkness
toward the next fragile man.

49

January mornings rise out of the prairie
slowly, knowing the accumulation of hours
cannot expel grayness,

and we become these hours,
tending to each pale breath,
a piece of ourselves swallowed by cold.

Even Sadie Miller feels her feet flex,
buried beneath tattered quilts,
waiting for the crack of shells
under snow that has compacted and inhaled,
waiting for the rush of toes
blinking against wool when the air seeps in
through unstitched spaces.

These are hours to settle into.
Search for the swirling of steam
exhaled against the muted miles,
and remain a warm contrast
to a morning that stains the inside.

50

Yellow sheets and a dead ant
on the windowsill
invite me to another Sunday,
a day that Downer sleeps.

We sometimes chuckle, recollecting the Sunday
Doug McKenzie had to wipe with an old shirt
after running out of toilet paper
because stores were closed, and dollars only moved
from wallets to church collection plates.

Sundays here isolate those who worship unassisted,
those who masturbate in their beds
with toes curled and legs straight,
those who chant breathlessness
with each steady wave through skin,
those who deepen desire to shut out
the constantly approaching light.

51

Every man meets a day
whose hours introduce to him
the beginning of seeing only peripheral colors
and the reality of a blurred grasp
around his own voice,

and these hours are smothered
by the tediousness of movement,
the flashes of faces meandering through aisles
of fragments for unsewn garments,

but there is a room in my basement,
walls lined with map murals,
and sometimes I run my fingers over mountains,
trace paths from Downer to Santiago
and west to Half Moon Bay
over oceans and wrinkles where the paper
didn't settle smoothly against the wall,
and I understand that if I cannot memorize
every name, elevation shift, and unintended tear
there is no reason to leave this room.

52

One man waits alone in a Fargo motel, staring
across the street while the white walled hospital
calls his wife away. He listens to hushed patterns
of brush strokes across the canvas,
trying to paint back their life.

Eighty-year-old child believing
his creation can somehow blot out her cancer.

Crimson barn where they taught their first son
to touch tongues with a baby cow,
turquoise car, fly-filled and manure scented
struggling up ditches and back to the house
after a day of twisting ears from stalks,
sky blue pond, as blue as her eyes and the dress
she wore, flowing in prairie breezes the first time
he knew.

January mornings rise out of the prairie
slowly, knowing the accumulation of hours
cannot expel grayness.

53

Today schools are closed and stores postpone transactions;
rows of tuna cans stand untouched,
and a colorful collection of deodorant rests in precise lines.
Everything waits while snow settles
in drifts over highways and gusts against doors,

but after the clouds pass through
and before streets are cleared and stores awaken,
Eve Miller turns the knob
and throws her weight against the door,
relocates the snow hill huddled against it,
and invites a whisper to rush through rooms
and a trace of snow to sit on her foyer floor.

She lives alone in a house of prudent decoration,
but today she finds sex in her front yard.
With red mittened hands she forms snow,
feels it soak through the yarn and sting her skin,
and as she forms the body her own heaves
rhythmically with the movement of snow,
and she pushes and pushes to know its pulse,
to work as one, to join woman and weather
and create a being of both, the snow-woman,

and after Eve has finished, she dresses snow in red mittens,
a blue wool coat and old black belt,
and she lies down, coatless and cold, beside the snow-woman,
clawing with naked hands for a thing
she knows she will never possess.

54

It's strange sometimes living
in such an unlit place.

I took a flight to Kansas City
out of Minneapolis once,
noticed the way the lights
spread from destination to destination,
wondered where the silence could hide
in all those grids of illuminated streets
and blinking towers.

55

Last week the annual cookbook
was released at the Methodist church,
and after the service women and men
waited patiently to see their names in print.

Phyllis Robbins brought her book home
and found her cashew calypso recipe
amidst a flurry of cream soup based hot-dishes.
She ran her fingers over the letters at the bottom,
imagining someday one of the books
would somehow reach a used bookstore in New York,
and a woman there might make her recipe,
see her name, and taste a piece of her life.

56

Lives here are snowflakes balancing on branches
after the storm has passed through,
and only the occasional gust can remove us.

Tonight Seth Madsen trudges across my window
in his old red coat, not minding that it's after midnight,
unconcerned with what the neighbors might say,
only compelled with making temporary foot-prints,
moving faster than the snow can fill his life.

He waits for a wind that will carry the flakes
that have been resting on tree boughs
across his path and into the unknown night.

Tonight he is the only one to follow this path
of Christmas lights and lamp posts from house to house,
and he endures the sting of snow on his neck
in that space where hat and coat don't quite meet,

but as I turn up the thermostat again
and put an extra blanket on the bed,
I know his searching is better than my warmth.

57

Estella Roberts spent three years teaching in Tulsa
and now says that sometimes after a long trip
the only feeling you remember
is that of going home,
as though home were the true place of travel,

but she did take with her
waves of children's laughter,
the smell of fresh flour tortillas,
and a river her eyes could not consume.

Now these flashes rest under her tongue,
a place to touch only when the sting of cold
can no longer be felt,
only when home itself is no longer
a true place of travel.

Crimson barn where they taught their first son
to touch tongues with a baby cow.

58

Jazz music does not live here.
The music of Downer is a church hymn
played slightly out of step with its intended rhythm
on the keys of an out of tune piano
and always a little too loud and a little too slow.

The wood thrush does not live here.
The birdsong of Downer is the squawking goose,
so familiar in his routine here that he's stopped flying south
and plods across snow covered pastures
waiting for the land to live again.

Pop music stations don't get much play here.
Instead Downer radio dials rest on the full bellies of tired tunes
and the a.m. stations that advertise yard sales
and constantly call out the local weather report,

but most days I keep the radio off
and stand silent with feet firmly fixed
on the worn rug behind the register,
not hearing the tired requests of customers
but responding anyway
as I listen to only the ticking of the clock overhead
and the muted drumming of a dead pencil on paper
and the steady hum of the long lament of loneliness.

59

Sometimes clarity collects itself in bursts,
but a day is never enough to hold the ambitions
that come to a man after too many waking hours
when he finds old scraps of sentences written
on yellowed paper, praise from third grade teachers
and the stray Valentines the years found worth saving,

and he forgets the smell of his mother's wedding dress,
the burning yellow mass and smoke curling to clouds
the week after her death when no one else could make
a decision, item to item thrown in one pile or the other,

and he returns to his fabric store hours after closing
to drape satin and taffeta over his nose and eyes,
to know the freshness of a wedding dress before burning,
and find her face somewhere in the white masses
but make it only fabric again before leaving.

60

Karen Larson is in her last year
teaching health and history and sometimes art
to children and teenagers at our tiny rural school.

Outside it is raining,
and minds in classrooms are clicking on,
each room housing a few
who will carry the knowledge forward,
lines from poems and geometry proofs
scribbled across dusty chalkboards
and transferred over to notebooks and memories,

and for now she still stands at the front,
trying to touch the depths of one mind,
even for a moment,
before hers has expired.

61

One man never learned to ride a bike.
He looks out his window
at children with scraped knees
and blows breath on their cuts
which fogs up the glass.

He stares back at years
too proud to fall,
too poisoned with the idea
of pain, pebbles from pavement
thrust under skin,
to feel the rushing light
of movement, of seeing.

62

My morning walk finds a bloody pad
beside yellow grass in the ditch.
I stop a moment to watch
a newly formed colony of ants
scurrying over the cotton-ball surface,
into the stained center

and wonder if the woman
was as beautiful as this.

Pop music stations don't get much play here.
Instead Downer radio dials rest on the full bellies of tired tunes
and the a.m. stations that advertise yard sales
and constantly call out the local weather report.

63

Watching the cars
wait for a train
was maybe the most painful thing
that happened today.

There is never a separation
between pleasure and hesitation.

Even that constant clanging
could have been music.

64

As trees reject their offspring,
losing their grasp a little more every day,
the descendants fade and fall
and eventually decompose into the mud,
unrecognizable by the time spring arrives.

I notice the fly dead between the window panes,
look at him and know his grief—
nowhere to go.

Charlene chose a ring,
showed it to the others and then me.
She danced through my hallways
and kitchen, singing wedding hymns
and said she wished
she could have told my mother.

I can see my life before
and the one I imagined,
but unseen walls
keep me here,
so I'll fly madly around
until I tire and hit the ground.

I'll breathe slowly at the window's bottom for a while;
time will pass;
my dreams will die.

65

The summer I turned twenty-two
Fae Williams worked at Sundae Dreams,
so I fell in love with frozen foods
to see the girl with the ice cream smile.

Once, while ordering, I asked her
if she could make my three dollars in change
quarters, just to stand there longer
and ask which flavor she liked best.

This summer while Charlene fills the freezer
with exotic flavors—papaya pecan,
peanut butter cheesecake, and snicker doodle pie—
I remember Fae saying gracefully, "Vanilla."

66

In the life I didn't choose
it is not my wedding day,
and I am proud of myself
for the escape or the rejection I created
and for the words I didn't say,

and in this other life
each hour is not pulling me
closer to becoming the man scratching the edges
of years inside a dull painting,
and time stretches before me still
like rural roads running over wide plains,

but in this other life Charlene is not
smiling as a stranger forms her hair
into those symmetrically standard curls she often gushes about,
and she doesn't know the feeling of soft silk stretched carefully
across the layers of her skin and life,

so I'll pose politely for pictures
and nod and speak when asked to.
I'll kiss and dance and eat the lemon cake Charlene chose
because maybe in the end it's all the same,
and it doesn't really matter when
life stops.

67

The wedding came and went,
and maybe the morning I die
I'll tell the story to a crowded café,
of how Charlene snuck down the aisle
toward me, how I couldn't look at her,
how every decorated woman
sitting petaled seemed to sing to me
as Charlene moved silently to the sway
of a lonely violin.

Time stretches before me still
like rural roads running over wide plains.

68

Sometimes when the summer evening swells
and those still living strum guitars through open windows
and brushes soaked with hair are disrobed
and the breeze carries loose hair beyond yards for birds' nests,
sometimes when the house is so quiet I can hear
the silent strumming of grass blades brushing against each other
and words in books I used to know become the wind,
sometimes then I hear my mother's breath
rustling behind picture frames, still waiting
for the right moment to leave this town.

69

Downer holds those who never left.
While Fargo and Sioux Falls house those who did,
I remind this page of those who couldn't get out,
those who drag feet across these streets
and through the familiar desolation.

Searching for new sight is easy,
but a woman here learns to memorize
each crease of her eyelids
as Sunday folds into next March,
and Tuesday snows in another packed suitcase.

Ada Hanson's house fills with dust from gravel roads,
unspoken words tucked behind bookcases,
left behind when her daughter followed geese to Texas
twenty years before this night.

Tom Barrow sweeps the steps and dusts doorways
every June, remembering Father's Day
twenty-six years ago when Julie came back.
They ate strawberry pie, an afternoon he holds even now,
waiting all day on the old couch
for his daughter to walk through the door again.

Those who stay keep pieces
of places they will never go—
shell boxes purchased at Pamida,
steel figurines of the Eiffel Tower,
and Swedish crystal vases.

They spend year after year creating mementos
from a place no one will ever go—
a Christmas angel with hay hair
Herb made forty-nine years ago in Sunday school,
waiting by the window for a stranger
to drive by and remember her face.

www.ingramcontent.com/pod-product-compliance
Lightning Source LLC
Chambersburg PA
CBHW070001100426
42741CB00012B/3098